W9-BXU-343

21st Century
Basic Skills
Library

YOUR HEALTHY PLATE
FRUITS

by Katie Marsico

Cherry Lake Publishing • Ann Arbor, Michigan

3

CHERRY
LAKE
Publishing

Published in the United States of America
by Cherry Lake Publishing
Ann Arbor, Michigan
www.cherrylakepublishing.com

Content Adviser: Theresa A. Wilson, MS, RD, LD, Baylor College
of Medicine, USDA/ARS Children's Nutrition Research Center,
Houston, Texas

Photo Credits: Cover and page 1, ©Valentyn Volkov/Shutterstock, Inc.;
page 4, ©Beneda Miroslav/Shutterstock, Inc.; page 6, ©PhotoSky 4t
com/Shutterstock, Inc.; page 8, U.S. Department of Agriculture; page 10,
©Suprijono Suharjoto/Dreamstime.com; page 12, ©iStockphoto.com/
TatyanaGl; pages 14 and 20, ©Monkey Business Images/Shutterstock,
Inc.; page 16, ©iStockphoto.com/gchutka; page 18, ©Igor Dutina/
Shutterstock, Inc.

Copyright ©2012 by Cherry Lake Publishing
All rights reserved. No part of this book may be reproduced or utilized in
any form or by any means without written permission from the publisher.

Library of Congress Cataloging-in-Publication Data
Marsico, Katie, 1980–
    Your healthy plate. Fruits/by Katie Marsico.
        p. cm.— (21st century basic skills library. Level 3)
    Includes bibliographical references and index.
    ISBN 978-1-61080-346-5 (lib. bdg.)—ISBN 978-1-61080-353-3 (e-book)—
ISBN 978-1-61080-400-4 (pbk.)
    1. Fruit in human nutrition—Juvenile literature. 2. Fruit—Juvenile literature.
I. Title. II. Title: Fruits. III. Series.
    TX558.F7M37 2012
    641.3'4—dc23   2011034536

Cherry Lake Publishing would like to acknowledge
the work of The Partnership for 21st Century Skills.
Please visit *www.21stcenturyskills.org* for more information.

Printed in the United States of America
Corporate Graphics Inc.
January 2012
CLSP10

TABLE OF CONTENTS

What Are Fruits?

Do you like crunchy apples? How about sweet cherries?

These foods are **fruits**.

Fruits grow after a plant's flower fades. The fruit is the plant's seed holder.

Farmers grow many different kinds of fruit.

Some farmers grow **citrus** fruits such as oranges.

Other farmers grow berries or melons.

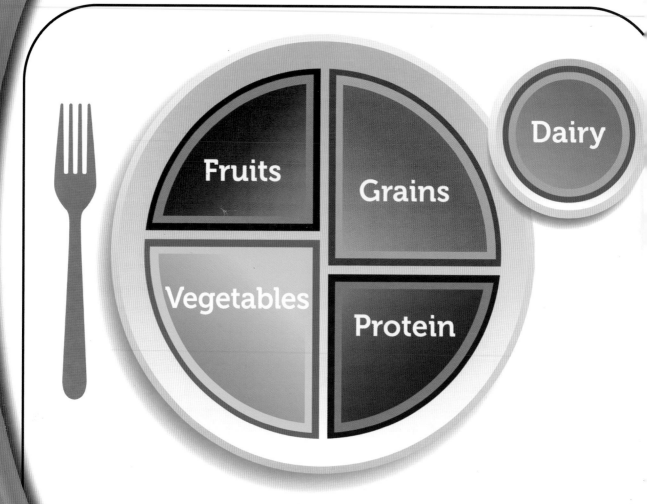

ChooseMyPlate.gov

Why Do You Need Fruit?

Fruits are one of five main **food groups**. All five groups should be part of your diet.

Eating a **balanced diet** is important. It will help you stay healthy and grow!

9

Why Else Should You Eat Fruit?

Eating fruit helps your body fight off illness. Fruit can help prevent many **diseases**.

Eating fruit can also help keep your heart healthy so it can do its job.

Many fruits have **vitamin C** in them.

This vitamin helps your body heal when you get hurt.

It keeps your teeth and eyes healthy, too!

How Often Should You Eat Fruit?

Someone your age should eat 1½ cups of fruit each day.

Fruits and vegetables should make up half of your plate at mealtime.

It is important to eat many different kinds and colors of fruits.

Each color of fruit has special ways to help your body grow healthy and strong.

Try mixing different **fresh** fruits together. You can make a fruit salad!

You can also drink fruit juice. Some people enjoy eating dried fruits such as raisins.

Talk to an adult about other ways to add fruit to your diet.

What fruits will you put on your plate today?

Find Out More

BOOK

Adams, Julia. *Fruits*. New York: PowerKids Press, 2011.

WEB SITE

United States Department of Agriculture (USDA)—Food Groups: Fruits
www.choosemyplate.gov/foodgroups/fruits.html
Learn more about fruit and how you can add it to your diet.

Glossary

balanced diet (BAL-uhntzt DYE-it) eating just the right amounts of different foods

citrus (SIH-truhs) a type of fruit that includes lemons, limes, and oranges

diseases (di-ZEEZ-uhz) conditions that cause health problems

food groups (FOOD GROOPS) groups of different foods that people should have in their diets

fresh (FRESH) not canned or frozen

fruits (FROOTS) parts of plants that often have seeds inside them and that can be eaten

vitamin C (VYE-tuh-min SEE) a substance found in fruit that helps the body heal and stay strong

Home and School Connection

Use this list of words from the book to help your child become a better reader. Word games and writing activities can help beginning readers reinforce literacy skills.

a	colors	foods	it	other	these
about	crunchy	fresh	its	part	this
add	cups	fruit	job	people	to
adult	day	fruits	juice	plate	today
after	diet	get	keep	prevent	together
age	different	groups	keeps	put	too
all	diseases	grow	kinds	raisins	try
also	do	half	like	salad	up
an	dried	has	main	seed	vegetables
and	drink	have	make	should	vitamin
apples	each	heal	many	so	ways
are	eat	healthy	mealtime	some	what
as	eating	heart	melons	someone	when
at	else	help	mixing	special	why
balanced	enjoy	helps	need	stay	will
be	eyes	holder	of	strong	you
berries	fades	how	off	such	your
body	farmers	hurt	often	sweet	
can	fight	illness	on	talk	
cherries	five	important	one	teeth	
citrus	flower	in	or	the	
color	food	is	oranges	them	

Index

About the Author

Katie Marsico is an author of nonfiction books for children and young adults. She lives outside of Chicago, Illinois, with her husband and children.